THE ART OF

ALPHA

MASTERING THE MINDSET OF
A SUCCESSFUL LEADER

Qurate
quratebooks.com

THE ART OF ALPHA
Prashant Mishra

First Edition: 2023

© Published by

qurate
quratebooks.com

Qurate Books Pvt. Ltd.
F-16, Alfran Plaza,
Opp. Don Bosco School,
Panaji - Goa India
Contact No: 18002106527
www.quratebooks.com

ISBN:978-81-19263-09-7
Printed at Manipal Technologies Limited, Manipal

To my dear parents and beloved brother, thank you for always being my rock, my support system, and my inspiration. This book is dedicated to you with all my love and gratitude.

Introduction

ALPHA is a mindset and qualities that can be found or developed in anyone irrespective of gender.

Why you need this book?

The majority of people worldwide actually have a faulty worldview because of their upbringing. Being an ALPHA person is related to this, too.

Additionally, they have been taught to view themselves as weak and untrue.

All of the significant issues we observe around the world are caused by this.
We observe that many people are unable to assume ownership of every aspect of their lives.

They are often seen acting the victim as they wait for the rest of the world to direct them and tell them what to do.
And if you consider the world as a whole right now, all of the instability and issues we observe in modern society may be linked to the general Beta attitude of most people. Because of this, issues like depression, divorce, anxiety, and people without direction are on the rise.

In contrast to the majority, the ALPHA Mind harnesses the innate urge for ALPHA thinking and transforms it into a potent ALPHA Mindset.

They accomplishes this by actively engaging in the mental and physical labour required to develop a potent mental environment, which involves recreating his worldview.

Recall that attitude is crucial.

The world takes notice of an ALPHA Mindset that has completely evolved.

A man with an ALPHA Mindset walks and talks in a certain way and uses unique, direct language.

His acts are deliberate, well-planned, and successful.

He sets an exemplary example and is a relentless achiever.

He knows the genuine nature of women and relationships on a personal level, and he also knows how to approach and handle committed relationships.

Can you get an ALPHA mindset overnight? No!

However, you may create an ALPHA attitude framework over the course of one night, after which you can start working to create and sustain that attitude.

It involves more than just one thing.

It involves applying a variety of actions learned from various information and wisdom sources steadily throughout time.

Over·time, one can cultivate and maintain an ALPHA attitude. A winning attitude is the ALPHA mindset.

The ALPHA Mindset is a lifestyle and a way of life.

I wrote this book to help all the one out there that are struggling in life or going through hard times, and feel like they are missing something but are not exactly sure what it is.

Let's take a look at what you can expect to see inside:

1. Why making a conscious decision to succeed in life.
2. How the mind machine functions.
3. How to rediscover your full potential as a man
4. Finding your life's purpose.
5. Who dares wins.
6. Risk and contemporary life.
7. The craft of caring for people.
8. Why you shouldn't seek for permission.
9. How to choose relationships wisely and

a whole deal more...

In this book you will learn about ALPHA personality in two sections
the very first you will know what exactly the ALPHA person mean And what are their qualities
In the latter section you will learn some techniques to adapt ALPHA traits in your day to day life.

Contents

Part 2 :- How to Be a Respectable ALPHA

Various techniques are given in this section to practice In day to day life

PART 1 :- DEFINATION AND QUALITIES OF ALPHA PERSONALITY

1. What is An ALPHA personality

An ALPHA person is the one who is highly intelligent, confident, and successful

A person who possesses these qualities is known as an ALPHA Person. ALPHA Person are typically seen as excellent leaders who seek to hold positions of authority. ALPHA Person frequently exhibit the following qualities:

1. being an authority figure
2. having no problem handling a lot of responsibility
3. liking to make the decisions
4. Possessing great degrees of influence and being the most impressive, successful, or powerful person in the room
5. Being self-assured and at ease with oneself, exercising restraint, being present, and believing that you are capable of handling anything are all characteristics of an ALPHA Person mindset.

In 100 bc the Greeks created their ALPHA bet, with the first letter being ALPHA . In the centuries that followed, the most dominant creature in a pack of wild animals (or supposedly more evolved humans) was ALPHA too.

Today's modern ALPHA Person doesn't need a finger test to pass muster. And here's some more groundbreaking info about real men today:

The old hard-line between ALPHA men and beta "nice guys" is blurry. ALPHA men are traditionally characterized as being unemotional and highly analytical, with little curiosity for others and their feelings. Men today are being encouraged to be knowledgeable about emotions and feelings, creating a new generation of strong, confident, and empathetic ALPHA Person leaders.

If you want to be a modern ALPHA Person, you need to aim high, elevate your brain and practice some ALPHA rule you will learn in this book.

Why Is an ALPHA Mindset Important?

The ALPHA attitude is crucial for success in both your personal and professional life. People with an ALPHA attitude are more likely to succeed in their occupations and in achieving their goals. A favourable influence on people around them is also more likely because they are more likely to be viewed as role models and leaders.

How to Develop an ALPHA Mindset

The good news is that over time, the ALPHA attitude can be created and nurtured. The following advice can help you develop an ALPHA mindset:

- **Increase your self-confidence**: The ALPHA mindset depends heavily on self-confidence. Start by concentrating on your accomplishments and strengths, and practise positive self-talk to develop your self-confidence.
- **Embrace assertiveness**: Aggression should not be confused with assertiveness, which is a crucial characteristic of ALPHA personalities.

Practise being courteous of others and being straightforward and direct when stating your thoughts and requirements.

Communicate effectively : Having an ALPHA mindset requires excellent communication. Engage in active listening, clear thought and emotion expression, and nonverbal communication.

2. Qualities of ALPHA personality

A. Developing Self-Belief : How to Trust Yourself and Your Capabilities

The ALPHA attitude revolves around self-assurance. It enables you to tackle difficulties with optimism and resiliency, and to have faith in your abilities and ability to overcome obstacles. The development of self-confidence and a strong feeling of self-belief will be the focus of this chapter's practical tactics.

• **Recognise your self-limiting thoughts**

Finding your self-limiting beliefs and challenging them is the first step to achieving self-confidence. These are the unfavourable ideas and opinions that limit your potential and keep you from reaching it fully. Consider the beliefs that are limiting you, and then utilise empowering affirmations and visualisation techniques to question and get rid of them.

• **Develop a growth mindset.**

The idea that you can learn and develop through effort and dedication is known as a growth mindset. Develop a growth mentality by accepting problems and viewing them as chances for development and learning. Celebrate your accomplishments along the road and keep your attention on the process rather than the result.

• **Embrace your own compassion**

The act of treating oneself with kindness and understanding is known as self-compassion. It entails treating yourself with the same compassion and support that you would extend to a friend, as well as accepting your mistakes and failings without passing judgement. By being friendly to yourself and praising your successes, you can develop self-compassion.

• **Practise empowering self-talk**

The act of talking kindly and encouragingly to oneself is known as positive self-talk. You may develop a positive self-image and increase your confidence by doing this. Positive affirmations and expressions of self-belief should take the place of negative self-talk, and they should be frequently practised.

• **Do Something**

Taking initiative is a crucial part of developing self-confidence. Make sure your goals are doable, then take baby measures to get there. Your confidence and belief in your skills and abilities will increase with each success and accomplishment.

• **Work on your visualisation skills**

Visualisation is an effective technique for boosting self-assurance. To visualise yourself attaining your goals and overcoming hurdles, use visualisation techniques. Use the image of a self-assured, successful person in your head to inspire and push yourself.

B. Leadership and Assertiveness: Taking Charge and Making Decisions

The boldness and leadership traits of the ALPHA personality are well-known. This chapter will discuss how to use assertiveness and leadership skills to take charge and make wise judgements.

- **Recognise the distinction between aggression and assertiveness**

Aggression and assertiveness are not synonymous. While assertiveness entails confidently expressing your wants and thoughts while respecting the needs and perspectives of others, aggression entails employing force or intimidation to obtain what you want. Use "I" statements, establish clear limits, and communicate with assurance and clarity to practise being assertive.

- **Improve Your Listening Skills**

Strong communication skills are necessary for effective leadership, and effective communication is a key component of active listening. To ensure understanding, engage in active listening by paying close attention to the speaker, seeking clarification, and paraphrasing what you have heard.

- **Exercise Making Decisions**

Leaders need to be capable of making judgements with assurance and rigour. Practise making decisions by dissecting complicated issues into simpler parts, acquiring pertinent data, taking into account a variety of viewpoints, and weighing the advantages and disadvantages of several possibilities before making a final choice.

- **Assign Responsibilities**

To ensure that activities are accomplished quickly and effectively, effective leaders assign duties and responsibilities to others. Leaders can concentrate on more important activities and strategic decision-making by delegating lower-level tasks. Practise assigning tasks to team members by noting their strengths and skills, setting clear goals and guidelines, and providing assistance and direction as required

• **Set a good example**

Leading by example inspires and motivates team members to provide their best effort. By setting a good example for your team, accepting accountability for your actions, exhibiting a strong work ethic, and being committed to excellence, you may lead by example.

• **Seek feedback and make improvements constantly**

Effective leaders are always looking for feedback and working to develop their competencies. Ask for input from teammates and peers, then utilise it to pinpoint areas for improvement and put changes into place that will make you a stronger leader.

C. Communication Skills: How to Express Yourself with Impact

A trait of the ALPHA personality is effective communication. In this chapter, we'll look at some useful tips and techniques for improving your ability to communicate effectively and express yourself powerfully.

• Acknowledge the Value of Nonverbal Communication

The way that people interpret your message can be greatly influenced by non-verbal cues including body language, tone of voice, and facial expressions. Pay attention to nonverbal signs and practise expressing confidence and assertiveness through your tone and body language.

• Become an expert at active listening

Effective communication depends heavily on active listening. Practise active listening by paying close attention to the speaker, seeking clarification, and expressing empathy and understanding to develop your communication skills.

• Develop Your Confidence and Clarity in Speaking

Effective communication relies heavily on confidence and clarity. Practise organising your thoughts before speaking, utilising direct language, and projecting your voice to talk with clarity and confidence.

• Address Your Audience with a Specific Message

Effective communicators recognise how crucial it is to customise their message for each audience. To make your message relevant and compelling, take into account the requirements, preferences, and viewpoints of your audience.

• **Use conflict resolution techniques**

Communication inevitably involves conflicts. Practise resolving conflicts by keeping cool and objective, paying attention to all points of view, and working cooperatively to come up with a compromise if you want to become a competent communicator.

• **Support Continuous Improvement and Feedback**

The finest communicators constantly look for criticism and work to develop their abilities. Ask for feedback from mentors and peers, then utilise it to pinpoint areas for growth and put new strategies into practise that will make you a better communicator.

D. Setting Goals and Achieving Them: Making Success Plans and Maintaining Focus

Setting lofty goals and pursuing them tenaciously are key success-enhancing skills that the ALPHA personality excels at. This chapter will cover useful techniques for establishing goals, coming up with a plan of action, and maintaining momentum towards your goals.

• Recognise the Value of Goal-Setting

Setting goals is the first step towards success. You can concentrate your attention and efforts on what really counts and boost your motivation and resolve to succeed by defining clear and defined goals.

Set **SMART** objectives.

SMART objectives are clear, quantifiable, doable, relevant, and time-bound. To make objectives clear and actionable, make sure they match these requirements when setting them.

• Create an action plan.

A plan of action lays out the measures necessary to accomplish your objectives. Make a timeframe for the fulfilment of your goals and break them down into smaller, more doable activities. You'll be able to stay motivated, organised, and focused using this.

• Retain Your Motivation and Focus

To achieve your goals, it's imperative to keep your motivation and focus high. Maintain attention by setting priorities for your tasks and frequently reminding yourself of your objectives. Celebrate your minor victories, ask for help from others, and visualise your triumph to stay motivated.

- **Overcoming Challenges**

Setting and achieving goals inevitably involves facing obstacles. Practise resilience and perseverance, get help and encouragement from others, and maintain a flexible and adaptive mindset to overcome challenges

- **Examine and correct**

You can stay on track and make the required modifications by periodically evaluating your progress and making changes to your plan of action. Determine what is and is not working, then adjust as necessary.

E. Managing Relationships : Gaining Others' Trust and Influence

The ALPHA personality is aware of the value of forging close connections and exerting influence over others. This chapter will look at several useful tactics for managing relationships well and gaining others' trust and influence.

• **Recognise the Value of Relationships**

Building relationships is crucial for success, both personally and professionally. You can win the confidence and support of people, create possibilities, and more successfully accomplish your goals by developing great relationships.

• **Exercise empathy and active listening**

Forging solid connections, active listening and empathy are essential. Practise active listening by paying close attention, exhibiting empathy, and trying to comprehend others' perspectives in order to gain their trust and influence.

• **Build Effective Communication Skills**

Building relationships with others requires effective communication abilities. Be confident and forceful, communicate clearly and effectively, and engage with others in an honest and open manner.

• **Create trust and credibility**

Building influence with people requires developing credibility and trust. Be reliable, follow through on commitments, and act and speak with honesty and consistency.

• Develop Win-Win strategies

In your interactions, finding win-win solutions can assist increase influence and trust. Find strategies to benefit both parties while attempting to comprehend their needs and interests.

• Effective Conflict Management

Any relationship will inevitably have conflict, and resolving it amicably is essential to gaining respect and power. Practise resolving conflicts by listening intently, attempting to comprehend all points of view, and working cooperatively to come up with a compromise.

F. Overcoming Obstacles: Resilience and Adaptability in the Face of Challenges

The ALPHA personality is aware that hurdles will inevitably appear and that success is not always simple. In this chapter, we'll look at useful techniques for overcoming hurdles, developing resilience, and adjusting to difficulties.

• Adapt to and welcome change.

The dominant personality understands that change is inevitable and that they must welcome it. Recognise that change presents possibilities for growth and development, and develop your ability to quickly adjust to new circumstances.

• Increase Your Resilience

Resilience is the capacity to recover from setbacks, and it is a crucial quality for achievement. Practise resilience by keeping a positive outlook, focusing on solutions rather than problems, and taking lessons from your errors.

• Maintain Attention on Your Goals

When faced with challenges, it's simple to lose sight of your objectives. Even in the face of difficulties, the ALPHA personality remains devoted to their goals and keeps their concentration on them.

• Do Something

The key to overcome barriers is to act. To move closer to your goals, divide larger goals into more manageable milestones and take persistent activity.

• **Enlist the Help of Others**

The ALPHA personality is aware that they need others to succeed. Seek out assistance from others, whether it be through networking, mentoring, or getting suggestions and direction from peers.

• **Take lessons from mistakes**

Failures and setbacks are unavoidable, but they can also present excellent chances for development and learning. Failures are opportunities for the ALPHA personality to grow, get better, and modify their winning techniques.

G. Understanding and Managing Your Own and Others' Emotions

An essential quality for the ALPHA personality is emotional intelligence. This chapter will discuss the significance of emotional intelligence and practical methods for comprehending and controlling both your own emotions and those of others.

• Comprehending emotional intelligence

The capacity to identify, comprehend, and control your own emotions as well as those of others is known as emotional intelligence. The ALPHA personality understands the value of emotional intelligence and how it contributes to success.

Awareness of Oneself

The basis of emotional intelligence is self-awareness. The ALPHA personality is conscious of their feelings, abilities, limitations, and morals. They are able to comprehend how their emotions and actions affect both themselves and other people thanks to this self-awareness.

• Self-Control

The capacity to properly control your own emotions and reactions is known as self-regulation. The ALPHA personality engages in self-regulation by remaining composed under pressure, rephrasing unfavourable thoughts, and restraining their emotions.

• Compassion

The capacity to comprehend and relate to the feelings of others is known as empathy. The ALPHA personality demonstrates empathy by paying attention to what others have to say, taking into account their viewpoint, and genuinely caring about their welfare.

• **Social Awareness**

The capacity to engage and communicate effectively with people is known as social skills. The ALPHA personality develops social skills by establishing trusting connections, speaking up and being forceful, and finding constructive solutions to issues.

• **Develop mindfulness**

Being mindful means paying attention to the present moment and the work at hand. The ALPHA personality practises mindfulness by maintaining goal-focus, being aware of their emotions, and scheduling time for self-care.

H. Developing a Growth Mindset and Lifelong Learning Habits: Ongoing Learning and Growth

The dominant personality recognises the value of lifelong learning and development. This chapter will discuss the idea of a growth mindset as well as useful tactics for developing a habit of lifelong learning.

• Recognising the Growth Mindset

A growth mindset is the conviction that one's skills and intelligence can be improved through effort, commitment, and ongoing education. The growth attitude that the ALPHA personality adopts acknowledges that intelligence is not fixed but may be increased with effort.

• Promoting the Growth Mindset

It takes deliberate work and repetition to develop a development mentality. Setting objectives, accepting challenges, asking for feedback, and viewing failures as teaching moments are all ways that the ALPHA personality fosters a growth attitude.

• Make Learning a Habit for Life

For the ALPHA personality to continuously develop and progress, it is imperative that they form a habit of lifetime learning. The ALPHA personality makes time for learning, reads frequently, goes to seminars and workshops, and looks for coaches and mentors.

• **Take lessons from mistakes**

Failure is a chance for growth and learning. Failure is not feared by the ALPHA personality since they view it as a good learning opportunity. They take stock of their mistakes, pinpoint areas for development, and apply this knowledge to future choices.

• **Adapt to Change**

Since change is unavoidable, the ALPHA personality welcomes it as a chance to advance. They are open to new concepts, viewpoints, and experiences and are prepared to take measured risks to accomplish their objectives.

· **Support others' growth**

The ALPHA personality values helping others develop. They mentor and coach others, impart their experience, and offer chances for others to learn and advance.

I. The ALPHA Lifestyle: Finding the Right Balance Between Work, Health, and Relationships for Success and Fulfilment

The ALPHA personality is aware that happiness and success stem from leading a balanced life that puts a strong emphasis on relationships, health, and work. We will discuss the significance of striking a balance in these areas as well as doable methods for doing so in this chapter.

- **Setting work priorities**

The ALPHA personality is aware of how crucial work is to success and happiness. By establishing specific objectives, making a schedule, concentrating on their most crucial activities, and avoiding distractions, they prioritise their work.

- **Maintaining Physical Health**

In order to accomplish their goals and keep up their high level of energy and attention, people with an ALPHA personality need to maintain their physical health. They put their health first by following a nutritious diet, getting regular exercise, getting enough sleep, and attending to their mental health.

- **Fostering Relationships**

The ALPHA personality needs to nurture relationships if they want to be fulfilled and happy in their lives. By prioritising their relationships, they spend quality time with their loved ones, communicate clearly, and forge deep bonds.

• **Stress management**

For the ALPHA personality to stay in balance and avoid burnout, stress management is crucial. By putting self-care first, emphasising relaxation techniques, and developing the ability to say no when required, they prioritise stress management.

• **Having a healthy work-life balance**

The ultimate aim of the ALPHA lifestyle is work-life balance. By establishing limits, prioritising their time, assigning responsibilities, and taking time for themselves, the ALPHA personality maintains a healthy work-life balance.

• **Adopting a growth-oriented mindset**

The ALPHA personality needs to adopt a growth mentality in order to stay in balance and keep getting better. By accepting difficulties, learning from mistakes, asking for criticism, and forming lifetime learning habits, they place a priority on progress.

Part 2 :- How to Be a Respectable ALPHA

1.Confidence

For an ALPHA person, confidence often refers to a strong belief in oneself and one's talents, a sense of self-assurance, the capacity to take calculated risks, and the ability to deal with difficulties in a cool, collected manner.

ACTION STEPS : FAKE IT UNTILL YOU MAKE IT

strategies to boosting your self-assurance in the real world:

1. Determine your strengths and emphasise them.

2. Set and work towards reasonable goals.

3. Adopt an optimistic approach and frame of mind.

4. Be surrounded by encouraging individuals.

5. Take advice from your mistakes and failures.

6. Maintain your physical and emotional well-being.

7. Practise forgiveness and self-compassion.

8. Take on difficulties, and go beyond your comfort zone.

9. Become open to learning and cultivate a growth mentality.

10. Maintain a positive body language and posture.

11. Be assertive and speak up in a polite way.

12. Use empathy and active listening.

13. Look for fresh chances and experiences.

14. Exercise introspection and self-reflection

15. Maintain organisation and set wise time priorities.

16. Use visualisation and affirmation strategies.

17. Accept accountability for your choices and actions

18. You should be accountable for your choices and actions.

19. Confront your worries and your inadequacies.

20. Celebrate your achievements and victories.

Have confidence in your abilities.
There is no quick fix or one size fits all answer; keep in mind that developing confidence is a long process. You will gradually get more assurance and self-assurance if you continuously put these suggestions into practise and are patient with yourself.

2. maintain a positive reputation and strong personal brand as a person

Research recommends that keeping a positive standing areas of strength for and brand is fundamental for progress in both individual and expert life. A solid individual brand can improve your validity, draw in potential open doors, and construct entrust with others. To keep a positive standing areas of strength for and brand, it is vital to reliably exhibit characteristics like uprightness, trustworthiness, and dependability. Making and sharing great substance, organizing with others, and effectively dealing with your internet based presence can likewise help construct and keep a positive standing. Furthermore, getting a sense of ownership with botches, being available to criticism, and consistently working on oneself can assist with hardening areas of strength for a brand over the long haul.

Action steps: Always stay true to your words.

1. Stay true to who you are and what you stand for.

2. Always conduct yourself honourably and honestly.

3. Show consideration and kindness to others.

4. Express your gratitude and appreciation to those that assist and support you.

5. Be happy and upbeat

6. Accept accountability for your choices and actions.

7. Actively listen while communicating clearly.

8. cultivate enduring connections with others.

9. Be dependable and trustworthy.

3. Similar Nodding

ALPHA align their nodding with their remarks to convey to others that they are very confident. They might nod their head and say, "Yes," or "I agree," for instance. And if they disagree, you might see them shake their heads and say, "No."

ALPHA nod not only as they speak but also as they listen.

Researchers discovered that when someone nods at us, we tend to speak 3–4 times longer. Why?

Because he can express both his viewpoint and his empathy by nodding. He will nod in agreement and will also nod "No" when he empathises with someone else ("That's terrible!"). Shepard finds that nodding fosters relationships and gives people a sense of belonging.

Nod with your words while speaking and while listening

few examples of typical nods during conversation:

1. Simple up-and-down nods are made by tilting the head gently up and down in response to a query or statement. It
may imply acceptance, comprehension, or acknowledgment.

2. Nodding from side to side, usually while hearing someone else talk, is known as a side-to-side nod. It may inspire the speaker to continue by indicating interest or curiosity.

3. Two fast nods followed by a third can be used to express emphatic agreement or enthusiasm.

4. **Slow nod:** A slow, deliberate nod may be used as a sign of reflection or deep thought, indicating that the speaker is giving the other person's words considerable consideration.

It's important to keep in mind that nodding styles can differ across situations and cultures, therefore it's crucial to be conscious of cultural conventions when speaking with people from other backgrounds.

4. Comforting Touch

According to studies, charismatic ALPHA males touch others more than they touch themselves. They exhibit self-touch indications that are less tense, such as:

the person's neck
clenching their fists
rubbing their arm

Instead, they are always looking for comforting touches from others:

High-fives
Thank yous and hugs
A comforting shoulder tap

Because they are a nonverbal "I understand you" signal, reassuring touches are wonderful.

Use touch to reassure, calm, or recognize people.

The following eight reassuring touch kinds can be used during a conversation:

1. **Hand on the forearm:** Putting one's hand on another person's forearm can be a comforting sign of support, especially when giving advice or expressing sympathy.

2. Gently massaging someone's shoulder can help them relax and show support, especially when they're feeling stressed or concerned.

3. A soft pat on the head can be a calming gesture, especially when providing assurance or motivation.

4. **Side hug:** When someone is feeling sad or vulnerable, a side hug can be a supportive gesture of comfort and encouragement.

5. **Back rub:** Particularly when someone is worried or overwhelmed, a gentle back rub can assist release tension and elicit support.

6. **Holding hands:** When someone is stressed out or disturbed, holding their hand can be a very effective approach to comfort and support them.

7. **Full grasp:** When someone is going through severe emotional anguish, a full embrace can be a powerful method to show comfort and support.

8. **Pat on the back:** In instances where someone is sad or emotional, a soft pat on the back can be a comforting sign of support and encouragement.

Once more, it's crucial to keep in mind that a reassuring touch should always be appropriate for the circumstance and voluntary. It's crucial to respect others' personal space as well as cultural restrictions on physical contact.

5. Visionary thinking

Visionary reasoning is the capacity to envision and anticipate a superior future, expecting changes and finding a way proactive ways to make that vision a reality.
It includes having a reasonable feeling of direction, an eagerness to face challenges, and the capacity to rouse and inspire others towards a common objective.

The following are moves toward foster visionary reasoning:

1. Foster a reasonable feeling of direction and long haul objectives.

2. Participate in essential wanting to distinguish open doors and possible snags.

3. Develop an inquisitive and open outlook to remain creative and ground breaking.

4. Encircle yourself with different viewpoints and search out new encounters.

5. Remain informed about industry patterns and changes.

6. Foster areas of strength for an of counselors and coaches.

7. Proceed with carefully thought out plans of action and gain from disappointments.

8. Use innovativeness and creative mind to produce novel thoughts.

9. Convey your vision plainly and enthusiastically to other people.

10. Urge and engage others to add to the vision.

11. Remain fixed on the higher perspective and don't get hindered in subtleties.

12. Embrace change and adjust rapidly to new conditions.

13. Gain from past victories and disappointments.

14. Celebrate little wins and use them as inspiration to continue onward.

15. Foster a need to get moving to get things going.

16. Take responsibility for vision and be responsible for results

17. Stay persistent and don't give up when faced with obstacles.

18 .Be adaptable and willing to pivot if necessary.

6. Taking Up Space

A person's demand for space increases with their level of confidence:

Using armrests
their arms encircling a couch stance
with the feet widely spaced
Samuel Jackson takes a seat on the couch and establishes his territory.

Space is also available for you! But be careful not to assert your space in an aggressive or forceful manner. ALPHA s do this because they feel at ease in circumstances where others might feel uneasy.

The ALPHA at the table may even be seen occupying the boss's seat.

When you feel confident, claim your space.

During a conversation, occupying some physical space can make you come across as aggressive and self-assure

Here are a few techniques to do it:

1. Standing tall means keeping your back straight, shoulders tucked in, and head held high. This stance exudes confidence and power.

2. Take up space by separating your feet and placing your feet firmly on the ground. This exudes a feeling of security and command.

3. Use hand gestures to draw attention to your arguments and occupy more space. This may make you seem more enthusiastic and assured.

4. **Maintain eye contact:** Look the other person in the eye while you're speaking. This gives off a sense of assurance and facilitates bonding.

5. **Speak clearly:** Make sure your voice is loud and clear. This exudes assurance and power.

6. **Avoid fidgeting:** Fidgeting and arm crossing can give the impression that you are defensive or closed off.

7. Lean in slightly to the person you're speaking to in order to show interest and involvement.

It's important to remember that taking up physical space should not be done in a way that makes others feel uncomfortable or intimidated. It's important to be respectful of others' personal boundaries and cultural norms around physical space.

7. Eye Openness

People who lack self-assurance or are not ALPHA tend to close up; they could cover their chest with an arm or keep something near to it. ALPHA s, in contrast, sit, stand, and stroll in a public manner.

To inspire openness, show openness.

Keeping your eyes open and your mouth open throughout a conversation can show respect, curiosity, and interest. Following are some pointers for keeping your eyes open throughout a conversation:

Make eye contact: Look the person in the eye as you speak to them. This demonstrates your curiosity and engagement with what they have to offer.

While it's crucial to maintain eye contact, try to avoid staring too intently, as this may make the other person feel uneasy.
Look away occasionally: During a conversation, it's normal to look away occasionally. By doing so, you can avoid staring and project attentiveness.

Eye contact is a powerful way to demonstrate interest. This can be done by nodding, grinning, or expressing interest in the discourse with your face.

Be conscious of cultural norms: When speaking with people from diverse backgrounds, it's crucial to keep in mind that eye contact can indicate different things in other cultures.

A conversation should not be interrupted by gazing around the room or checking your phone. This may imply disdain or disinterest.

Be present: Concentrate on the current discussion and make an effort to be totally in the present. By doing so, you can remain alert and demonstrate your appreciation for the other person's time and opinions.

8. Invites Others to Participate

Even in adverse conditions, ALPHA men ask others to participate!

ALPHA person doesn't lose his cool or become extremely enraged. He really takes the person who splashed water in his face by the hand and asks, "What's so funny about this?" to gain control of him.

It's entrenched to act in this way. Even in difficult circumstances, they are accustomed to bringing individuals in and getting answers.

Take charge by inviting others to participate more.

The ability to include people in a conversation is crucial for fostering inclusivity and involvement

Here are some strategies for inviting people to join a conversation.:

1. **Ask open-ended questions**: Make inquiries that call for more information than a simple affirmative or negative response, and invite respondents to express their opinions.

2. **Use inclusive language**: Ask questions like "what do we all think about this?" or "does anyone have any other ideas?" that include everyone in the discussion.

3. **Listen actively**: Actively hear what others have to say, and then prompt them to elaborate by posing follow-up questions.

4. **Show interest**: Show interest in what others are saying by nodding, making eye contact, and engaging with their ideas.

5. **Avoid interrupting**: Give others a chance to finish their sentences before reacting when they are speaking.

6. **Encourage participation**: Make sure everyone feels comfortable sharing their ideas by directly requesting them to do so and by establishing a safe and supportive environment.

7. **Summarise and reflect**: To demonstrate that you value others' opinions and are paying attention, summarise what others have said and reflect it back to them.

Keep in mind that requesting people to speak should be done in a polite and suitable way so as not to make them feel uncomfortable or under pressure to do so.

9. Humility

Humility means being free of pride or arrogance and not acting like you're better than others. ALPHA didn't achieve true happiness and success until he chose humility:

there's no secret to humility.
Work hard, stay hungry, and never behave like a stereotypical dominant ALPHA male.
Remember: the only thing a modern ALPHA male ever beats into submission is his ego.

You also don't have to keep your vulnerabilities a secret.
Being an ALPHA male is not about being perfect.
Your mistakes are a learning experience.
When you make a mistake, lose your temper, or misbehave, own it and learn from it.

Don't be afraid of authenticity.
If you're unsure of yourself, your reservations or lack of confidence may seem arrogant.

Your authentic pride comes with self-esteem and seeing yourself as valuable but not superior to others.
ALPHA males focus on achieving, but they're agreeable and attuned to the thoughts and feelings of others.

Eight techniques for increasing humility:

1. **More listening:** Pay attention to what other people are saying and make an effort to comprehend them without interrupting or minimising them.

2. **Accept suggestions:** Even negative input should be welcomed since it might help you become a better person.

3. **Admit mistakes:** Accept responsibility for your actions when you are mistaken or have committed an error.

4. **Avoid boasting:** It might come off as arrogant, so refrain from talking excessively about your successes or bragging about them.

5. **Embrace gratitude:** Be appreciative of others' contributions and efforts while being thankful for what you have.

6. **Be teachable:** Keep an open mind to new information and be prepared to acknowledge your ignorance in a subject.

7. **Serving others** is putting others' needs ahead of your own, as well as working towards the common good.

8. **Practise empathy** by putting yourself in others' situations and making an effort to comprehend their feelings and experiences while also being nice and compassionate to them.

10. Use a Variable Tone of Voice (and Volume)

ALPHA s have been discovered to have dynamic voices. When they are impassioned, they speak louder, and when something is significant, they speak quietly. Alternately, they speak quickly during a story and more slowly during a point.

Some also makes a large, bold, and low splash. That is fantastic in ALPHA s! However, not all ALPHA s have to be as large and imposing . Some people, like Brad Pitt, can be quiet yet confident.

Note : Use lots of vocal variety and dynamic volume

Here are some examples of how to employ a varied tone of voice in conversation:

1. **Change your voice's pitch** to emphasise certain words or phrases by varying your pitch. Your pitch can communicate excitement or enthusiasm when it is raised or urgency when it is lowered.

2. **Increase or decrease your voice loudness** to convey various feelings and meanings. Speaking softly might suggest closeness or weakness, whilst speaking aloud can suggest power or authority.

3. **Use inflection:** Accentuate certain words or phrases, and use inflection to convey various feelings and meanings. A statement or phrase's meaning can be altered by stressing or emphasising particular words.

4. **Use pauses** to add emphasis and communicate significance to your words. A little pause before or after a crucial point might assist highlight it and give it additional weight.

5. **Match the tone:** Adapt your voice's inflection to the circumstance and the listener. Speaking in a soothing or calming tone, for instance, can make someone feel better if they are unhappy.

6. **Be conscious of your body language**: Your body language can affect the tone of your voice, so pay attention to how your posture, gestures, and facial emotions may be impacting your tone.

7. **Active listening** is a skill that can help you respond to the other person's tone and emotions correctly and change your own tone to fit it.

Just keep in mind that doing so in a respectful and proper way is important to avoid coming off as manipulative or insincere.

Ten different sorts of changing tones of voice are listed below that you can employ during a discussion to express various feelings and meanings:

1. To express passion and excitement, raise your voice's pitch and volume.

2. **Empathy:** To express empathy and understanding, use a softer, more soothing tone of speech.

3. **Seriousness**: To project a sense of gravity and seriousness, use a lower tone and a slower speed.

4. **Humor**: Use a playful tone of voice with exaggerated inflections to convey a sense of humor and lightheartedness.

5. **Authority**: Use a firm, assertive tone of voice to convey a sense of authority and confidence.

6. To convey a sense of urgency and importance, speak at a faster pace and with a more urgent tone of voice.

7. To indicate sarcasm, use an exaggerated or contradictory tone of voice to the words being uttered.

8. To demonstrate curiosity and a willingness to learn, use an inquiring and enthusiastic tone of voice.

9. **Sadness**: To express sadness and empathy, speak in a softer, slower tone of voice.

10. To express thanks and thankfulness, use a tone of voice that is warm and grateful.

Remember, the tone of voice you use should match the situation and your intentions, and should always be used in a respectful and appropriate manner.

11. Gaze More (Especially at the End of a Statement)

Generally speaking, ALPHA s make more eye contact, but especially at the conclusion of sentences. ALPHA s may be thinking as they speak, but in the end, they may want to know how you feel.

ALPHA s don't always feel the need to make eye contact, but they do it when they want to emphasise a point or assess how people are responding.

Gaze more, especially at the end of statements.

Different kinds of gazes might be exchanged throughout a discourse. Here are a few illustrations:

1. **Direct gaze:** This occurs when a speaker maintains eye contact with the listener. It can imply assurance, fascination, and engagement.

2. **Averted gaze:** This is when a speaker avoids making eye contact with the listener. It may suggest unease, timidity, or dishonesty.

3. **Glancing gaze:** This is the act of looking at the person you are speaking to for a split second before looking away. It can imply shyness, anxiety, or disinterest.

4. **Staring gaze**: This occurs when someone keeps their eyes fixed on the person they are speaking to for a long time. It might imply dominance, intimacy, or aggression.

5. When someone is chatting to someone, they may cast a sideways gaze their direction. It can imply mistrust, scepticism, or apathy.

6. When someone speaks while looking up, this is known as an upward gaze. It can imply reflection, thinking, or ambiguity.

7. When someone stares down while speaking, it is known as a downward gaze. It can imply modesty, melancholy, or shyness.

It's vital to keep in mind that standards and expectations for eye contact and gazes during conversation may vary among cultures and social circumstances. As a result, it's critical to pay attention to cultural and social cues and modify your own behaviour accordingly.

12. More Hand Gestures

ALPHA males use a lot of their hands to explain their words. They underline or bold their words with their hands with purpose and impact.

And a great example of an ALPHA male who uses a lot of hand gestures is The Rock. He uses hand gestures expertly, as well as a handful of other cues that makes him ALPHA .

Ten frequent hand motions that are used during discussion are listed below:

1. When you point, you extend your index finger to signify a specific object or direction.

2. **Open palms:** When your palms are facing outward, it can be interpreted as being receptive, honest, and open.

3. **Handshake:** This is the customary greeting and expression of agreement in which you take hold of someone else's hand with your own.

4. **Thumbs up/down:** This is when you extend your thumb up or down to indicate approval or disapproval..

5. **Clenched fist:** This is when your hand is made into a fist and is used to express resolve, rage, or frustration.

6. When you pinch something, you can imply precision or smallness by using your thumb and index finger to grip it.
7. An expression of attention or absorption can be conveyed by stroking or massaging your chin with your fingers.

8. Nodding is the act of moving your head up and down to express agreement or comprehension.

9. **Shoulder shrug:** When you raise your shoulders towards your ears, it can be seen as lack of knowledge or uncertainty.

10. When you wave your hands back and forth, you can say hello, goodbye, or dismiss someone.

hand gestures can vary greatly across cultures, and what may be appropriate or common in one culture may not be in another. Therefore, it's important to be aware of cultural differences and to adjust your own behavior accordingly.

13. Perseverance

Perseverance means to keep on trying through challenges and difficulties. For example, here is a successful ALPHA billionaire who wouldn't have succeeded without perseverance:

Richard Branson started his first business at age 15. He eventually founded worldwide brands like Virgin Records, Virgin Gaming, Virgin Airlines, and Virgin Mobile. He even got knighted by a Queen!

Then, in 221, Branson took his ALPHA male game to outer space with the first spaceflight of Virgin Galactic. Branson's business empire is awe-inspiring, but he faced huge difficulties with Virgin Galactic that made him want to quit:

In July 27, a fatal explosion delayed the building of Virgin Galactic's rocket engines.

In October 214, Virgin Galactic's fourth rocket-powered test flight killed its copilot when the vehicle broke apart. If you think you can only learn perseverance through terrible moments and tragedies, Branson learned perseverance before he'd even made a dime.

Take a look at this
text:
"A fired who has dyslexia described to me how she eerpcexenis rdaeing. She can read, but it taeks a lot of creatnnoitocn, and the ltrtees smees to "jump aruond." I remibmeeed rniadeg aoubt tipmcylyogea. Wduoln't it be psbslioe to do it ietlvrciatney on a wibstee with Jpsiacarvt? Sure it wloud. Feel like miankg a bikoeorakmt of tihs or soinetmhg? Frok it on ghitub."

That's not a foreign language (or broken spell-check). Where others see normal-looking text, a person with the learning disability dyslexia sees this instead.

Richard Branson has dyslexia. It's why he failed at every subject in school and why his teachers wrote him off as an idiot bound for failure— or prison. But Branson persevered.

Researchers studying perseverance discovered that this mindset is essential in predicting long- term achievement. Here's how to build your perseverance.

Imagination is a powerful ALPHA trait, but don't stop there. Use it to make your dreams a reality.

Don't get angry when people doubt you. Instead, use grit (determination!) and follow your gut..

Here are ten strategies to develop more perseverance:

1. **Establish precise objectives:** Define your objectives precisely and divide them into smaller, more doable phases.

2. **Create a positive outlook:** Focus on your abilities and strengths rather than your weaknesses. Cultivate a positive attitude.

3. Develop self-discipline by making a strategy and following it even when you're unmotivated or encounter obstacles.

4. Create a network of support by surrounding yourself with positive influencers.

5. **Embrace challenges**: View challenges as opportunities to learn and grow, rather than as obstacles to overcome.

6. **Learn from failure**: Analyze what went wrong and use the lessons learned to improve your approach.

7. **Persist through setbacks**: Keep going even when you encounter setbacks or obstacles.

8. **Take calculated risks**: Step out of your comfort zone and take risks, but be prepared to learn from failure.

9. **Focus on the process**: Emphasize the journey rather than the destination, and celebrate small successes along the way.

10. **Believe in yourself**: Have confidence in your abilities and believe that you can achieve your goals, even in the face of adversity.

Remember, perseverance is not an innate quality, but rather a skill that can be developed and strengthened with practice and effort

14.Self-Control

Self-control is disciplining yourself over the impulses, emotions, or desires that aren't in your best interest.

Countless strategies exist for developing the pillars of self-control, including willpower, self-confidence, and balance. Self-control combines a "why" and "how" mindset.

• **Self-control means a "can-do" attitude.**

Academic research shows how self-control allows you to function better and deal with stress with a "can-do" attitude—when you believe that you can control yourself, you will.

Commit to motivating yourself.

Make a strong commitment to yourself, and motivate yourself to achieve what you want or deserve by controlling your life and reaching your goals— self- control drives you there.

Always know why.

Always keep a "why" mindset and use your passion to fuel your self-control.

how to exercise self control:

1. Practise mindfulness by being conscious of your thoughts, feelings, and actions right now.

2. **Delay gratification:** Put your long-term objectives ahead of your immediate desires and resist the need to act on them.

3. **Set objectives:** Create definite, defined objectives, then take steps to realise them.

4. **Make a strategy:** Create a plan of action to keep you on course and prevent rash choices.

5. Engage in meditation or deep breathing exercises to assist you manage stress and enhance your capacity for composure and concentration.

6. **Exercise:** Engaging in physical activity can help you relax, feel better, and have more self-control.

7. Ensure that you receive enough sleep because it can affect your judgement and self-control.

9. Self-talk that is constructive will help you to inspire and motivate yourself.

10. Seek support: Surround yourself with people who can keep you accountable and motivated while also supporting your ambitions.

15. Decision-Making

Decision-making is leading others in the act of deciding on important and complicated issues.

Control negativity and anxiety. Academic researchers have studied how anxiety and negativity impact anyone's ability to make a tough decision.

ways to make better decisions:

1. **Determine the issue**: The issue or issue you're attempting to fix should be clearly stated.

2. **Information gathering**: Compile all pertinent data and information about the issue.

3. **Think about alternatives**: Create many possibilities and weigh them

4. **Consider your options**: Consider each choice in light of factors including viability, effect, cost, and risk.

5. Sort the choices according to value or relevance to establish a priority.

6. **Make a choice:** Depending on your analysis and prioritisation, pick the best choice.

7. **Make a move**: Put your decision into action and carry out your plan of action.

8. **Follow developments**: Keep tabs on the development of your choice, evaluate it frequently, and make adjustments as needed.

9.Consider past errors as chances for learning and development by analysing them.

16. Goal-Oriented

Being goal-oriented means being purpose-driven to accomplish a task or succeed at an objective.

Ways to increase your goal-orientation

1. **Set your objectives**: Clearly define your objectives and set attainable, quantifiable goals.

2. **Detail your objectives**: To make your goals more attainable, break them up into smaller, more doable steps.

3. **Make a strategy**: Create a strategy for achieving your objectives and keeping track of your progress.

4. **Set deadlines**: To help you keep motivated and focused, set reasonable deadlines for each step of your plan.

5. **Prioritise**: Decide which objectives are most crucial, then arrange them in order of importance.

6. Take responsibility for your activities and hold yourself responsible for reaching your objectives.

7. Keep yourself inspired and motivated by reading inspirational quotes or surrounding yourself with inspiring people to help you stay on course.

8. **Assess and make changes**: To make sure you stay on track to meet your objectives, periodically evaluate your progress and make appropriate adjustments to your strategy.

17. Mental and Physical Strength

When most people think about being an ALPHA male, they think about being the strongest, biggest person in the room. However, strength is not just physical.

Being mentally and physically strong means your brain and body are aligned, whatever stage of life you're in.

methods to improve both physical and mental health:

• **Physical Fitness:**

1. Regular exercise can help you stay physically healthy, lower your chance of developing chronic conditions, and improve your mood.

2. Get enough sleep: To enhance physical well-being and lessen stress, aim for 7-8 hours of sleep each night.

3. Maintain a healthy diet by including a range of nutritious items in it, such as fruits, vegetables, whole grains, and lean proteins.

4. Drink enough of water all day long to stay hydrated and maintain healthy bodily processes.

5. To preserve good physical health, practise good cleanliness. Wash your hands frequently, brush your teeth twice a day, and take regular showers.

• **Mental Wellness:**

1. Self-care is the act of taking care of oneself. Examples of self-care include taking time to meditate, take a bath, or read a book.

2. **Seek assistance**: When you require emotional support, turn to friends, family, or a therapist.

3. Focus on the positive aspects of life and practise thankfulness by recognising and appreciating the positive aspects of your life on a regular basis.

4. Take part in hobbies you find rewarding an enjoyable, such as painting, cooking, or playing sports.

5. **Practise mindfulness:** Concentrate on the present experience rather than getting caught up in thoughts about the past or the future.

6. **Limit social media use:** Spend less time on social media to reduce comparison anxiety and enhance mental wellness.

7. **Get outside**: Spend time in the outdoors, such as on a walk or hike, to elevate your mood and lower your stress levels.

8. **Practise stress-management strategies**: To lessen stress, take part in exercises like yoga, deep breathing, or visualisation.

9. Hobbies are things you enjoy and find gratifying, such as painting, cooking, or participating in sports.

10. Establish healthy boundaries with others and learn to

say "no" to obligations or activities that you dont like.

11. For better mental health and to lessen feelings of loneliness or isolation, keep in touch with your friends, family, and neighbours.

Take Action because

ACTION IS WHAT MAKES YOU

AN Alpha ,

TALK IS CHEAP.